SONIA STEVENSON

Gourmet Salads

SONIA STEVENSON

Gourmet Salads

Photography by Simon Wheeler

WEIDENFELD & NICOLSON

Sonia Stevenson

Sonia Stevenson, a master chef for more than 25 years, founded and ran the Michelin-starred restaurant, The Horn of Plenty at Gulworthy in Devon. She has cooked as the visiting chef at many great restaurants, including Maxim's in Paris, where she was the first woman ever to do so.

She now devotes her time to passing on her considerable knowledge through teaching masterclasses, writing and appearing on television.

Her books *The Magic of Saucery* and *A Fresh Look at Fish* are best sellers. Her television appearances include BBC-TV's *Masterchef* and Granada's *More Calories Please*.

Contents

How many eloquent writers

feed the moths and bookworms,

when cooks alone can buy

their polished lines?

MARTIAL EPIGRAM 6.61
(Vol II, Loeb's Classical Library)

Introduction

Whether you are a restaurant chef or a home cook, you will always have your favourite recipes, but as fashions change and strange ingredients arrive in the supermarkets, so new dishes will be developed and presented in unfamiliar ways. Nowadays the word 'salad' embraces a range of styles and temperatures, from chilled food to hot morsels. This selection of salads combines the classic and the new, the fashionable and the foreign, but they have all been chosen for their individuality.

The majority of the ingredients are easy to find, and thanks to mail-order and specialist shops it is now possible to obtain items such as truffle oil and smoked duck without too much trouble.

Most of these dishes can be served as starters, and a few make main courses. Best of all, there is practically nothing to be done at the last minute, leaving you to enjoy a glass of something before putting them on the table. What could be easier?

Sophia Stevenson.

DUCK 'HAM' AND BLACK FIG SALAD

SERVES 4

1–2 magrets of duck*
3 tablespoons brandy
salt and pepper
8 figs

The thicker the duck breast, the more moisture it will retain once it is dried, but there will be some shrinkage.

Put the duck breasts in a bowl, add the brandy and turn the breasts until well moistened. Sprinkle with crushed sea salt and grind on some black pepper. Cover and refrigerate for 24–36 hours.

Place the duck breasts on a wire rack and leave in a cold oven with the fan operating for 3 hours or until a dry skin has formed on the meat. Alternatively, you could leave them on a rack in a cool, well-ventilated larder, blowing a cold hair-drier on them from time to time. Wrap them individually in muslin and hang them in a cool but not chilled place to dry for 10–14 days.

To serve, cut the figs across three times to make a flower shape, and sprinkle with salt and pepper. Slice the duck 'hams' very thinly and serve like Parma ham.

Serve as a first course, followed by osso bucco Milanaise.

AVOCADO, BASIL, FETA AND TOMATO SALAD

SERVES 6

4 tomatoes, skinned, seeded
   and diced
8–10 basil leaves, shredded
100 g/3½ oz feta cheese, diced
2–3 avocados

Dressing
½ tablespoon Dijon mustard
1 tablespoon red wine vinegar
4 tablespoons olive oil
pinch or two of sugar
salt and pepper

Mix the ingredients for the dressing together and season to taste.

Season the tomatoes lightly. Mix the tomatoes with the basil and feta and chill.

When you are nearly ready to serve, cut the avocados in half, remove the stones and peel, then slice or dice the flesh. Coat them with the dressing and then gently fold into the tomato mixture with as much of the dressing as necessary to coat well. Chill for up to 30 minutes – no longer or the avocado will blacken.

This makes a delicious light lunch, accompanied by crusty bread and a glass of white wine, followed with fresh fruit.

SALADE CAUCHOISE

SERVES 4

300 g/11 oz new potatoes
1 garlic clove, crushed
85 g/3 oz ham, cut into strips
1 fennel bulb, chopped, or
    2–3 sticks of celery
150 ml/5 fl oz double cream
½ lemon
½ bunch of spring onions, sliced
3 black olives, chopped

Dressing

½ tablespoon Dijon mustard
1 tablespoon white wine vinegar
6 tablespoons grapeseed oil
salt and pepper

Mix the ingredients for the dressing together and season to taste.

Boil the potatoes (with or without their skins) until just tender, then drain well. While the potatoes are still warm, mix them with the dressing and leave to cool.

Cut the potatoes into chunks and add the garlic, ham and fennel or celery.

Add the cream and some salt and pepper and mix well. Add a squeeze of lemon juice and mix very lightly, otherwise the cream will separate. Mix the spring onions with the olives and scatter over the salad.

Serve as an accompaniment to a duck terrine, or with cold roast pork with crackling. Follow with a hot apple charlotte and custard.

SALAD OF GREEN LENTILS
with quails' eggs

SERVES 4–6

olive oil for frying
2 slices of white bread, cut
    into cubes
8 slices of smoked streaky
    bacon
350 g/13 oz carrots, boiled
    in their skins
200 g/7 oz Puy lentils, cooked
    until just tender
5–6 fresh sage leaves, chopped
6 quails' eggs, hard-boiled,
    shelled and halved

Dressing

1 teaspoon Dijon mustard
1 tablespoon red wine vinegar
6 tablespoons olive oil
large pinch of sugar
salt and pepper

Mix the ingredients for the dressing together and season to taste.

Heat the olive oil in a frying pan, add the cubes of bread and fry until golden, then drain on paper towels.

Grill the bacon until dry and crisp, then crumble. Peel the carrots and finely dice. Put the lentils, sage, bacon and carrots in a bowl and mix with the dressing.

When you are nearly ready to serve, add the croûtons and decorate with the quails' eggs.

This is a substantial starter, or serve as an accompaniment to grilled gammon with french beans.

MEDITERRANEAN SQUID, SCALLOP AND CRAB SALAD

SERVES 4

5 tablespoons olive oil

5 shallots, chopped

4 tomatoes, skinned, seeded
   and chopped

150 ml/5 fl oz white wine

5–6 fresh basil leaves, chopped,
   plus extra to garnish

salt and pepper

vegetable oil for frying

6 small squid, cleaned and
   sliced

48 small 'queen' scallops

125 g/4 oz white crabmeat

1 small courgette

Heat the oil in a frying pan, add the shallots and sauté until soft. Add the tomatoes and white wine and simmer until all the liquid has evaporated. Add the chopped basil and season to taste with salt and pepper.

Heat the vegetable oil in a deep frying pan until very hot. Dip the squid and scallops into the hot oil a few at a time to seize them, but do not overcook. Lift out with a slotted spoon and drain on paper towels, then add to the tomato sauce. Add the crabmeat and chill.

Cut the courgette lengthways into ribbons, using a potato peeler. Reheat the oil and fry the courgette strips for a second or two; drain on paper towels.

Serve the seafood salad surrounded by courgette ribbons.

Follow with garlicky veal cutlets and mashed potatoes.

SPICED COUSCOUS

SERVES 6

3 tablespoons olive oil
½ tablespoon turmeric
½ tablespoon ground cumin
½ tablespoon ground ginger
4 whole cloves
½ stick of cinnamon
1 bay leaf
1 garlic clove, sliced
165 ml/5½ fl oz (measured in
   a jug) couscous
250 ml/8 fl oz hot chicken stock
salt and pepper
½ cucumber, peeled and finely
   diced
1 tablespoon chopped fresh mint
150 g/5 oz ready-to-eat dried
   apricots, chopped
100 g/3½ oz almonds, toasted
   and halved
50 g/2 oz pine kernels, toasted
100 g/3½ oz pecan nuts, roughly
   chopped
85 g/3 oz raisins
2 teaspoons clear honey

Dressing
1 tablespoon white wine vinegar
4 tablespoons olive oil
1 tablespoon clear honey

Mix the dressing ingredients together until smooth.

Heat the olive oil in a large frying pan, add the spices, bay leaf and garlic and fry together until the garlic is lightly browned, then mix in the couscous. Pour over the hot stock and stir over a low heat until the mixture swells and cooks, about 2 minutes. Remove from the heat, season to taste and keep stirring, off the heat, for a further 2 minutes, to free the grains. Stir in the dressing and leave to cool.

Remove the cloves if you can find them, and the cinnamon stick if you like.

Add the cucumber, mint, apricots, nuts, raisins and honey to taste.

Serve as an accompaniment to, or first course before, roast guinea fowl or chicken. Finish the meal with a piece of halva.

SAFFRON POTATOES
with orange segments and pickled walnuts

SERVES 4–6

large pinch of saffron strands
300 g/11 oz waxy new potatoes
2–3 sweet pickled walnuts,
    sliced
½ bunch spring onions, sliced on
    the diagonal
1 orange, segmented without
    pith or skin
1 tablespoon hazelnut oil
baby salad leaves
2 small heads of chicory,
    quartered
2 tablespoons white of leek,
    finely sliced

Dressing

½ tablespoon Dijon mustard
1 tablespoon white wine vinegar
6 tablespoons groundnut or
    grapeseed oil
salt and pepper

Mix the ingredients for the dressing together and season to taste.

Simmer the saffron strands in 300 ml/10 fl oz water to infuse. Scrape the skins from the potatoes and parboil them in plenty of boiling salted water. Drain and finish cooking them in the saffron water (leaving the strands in) until it is all absorbed. While the potatoes are still warm, mix them with the dressing and leave to cool. Chill overnight if possible.

To serve, slice the potatoes into rounds, add the walnuts, spring onions, orange segments and hazelnut oil. Pile on to a plate and surround with salad leaves and chicory. Scatter the leek rings over the salad.

Serve with cold roast beef and follow with a raspberry roulade or pavlova.

THAI LOBSTER SALAD

SERVES 4

2 cooked lobsters, about
   600 g/1¼ lb each
frisée, lambs' lettuce and
   radicchio
1–2 tablespoons light vinaigrette

Dressing

5 cm/2 inch piece of fresh
   ginger, sliced
200 ml/7 fl oz tinned coconut
   milk
grated zest of ½ lemon
½ green chilli (or to taste), sliced
1 tablespoon groundnut oil
salt and pepper

To make the dressing, finely slice a couple of pieces of the ginger into matchsticks and reserve for the garnish. Put all the ingredients in a small saucepan and simmer until thickened and the flavour has developed, about 10 minutes. Strain and leave to cool.

Cut the lobsters in half and remove the meat. Crack the claws and pick out the meat. Reserve the liver and the eggs, if there are any. Mix the liver with the cooled dressing, and use the eggs as a garnish for the claw meat. Pour the dressing over the lobster meat and chill until needed.

To serve, mix the salad leaves with the vinaigrette. Arrange the lobster meat and claw meat on a plate and surround with the salad leaves.

Serve as a main course with green salad and cold french beans. Follow with mangoes in a lime syrup.

Pasta salad
with truffle oil, Parmesan and trompettes de la mort

SERVES 4

50 g/2 oz fresh or 7 g/¼ oz
    dried trompettes de la mort
    (horn of plenty mushrooms)
½ lemon
2 tablespoons truffle oil
1–2 tablespoons grapeseed oil
salt and pepper
150 g/5 oz dried farfalle pasta
15 g/½ oz Parmesan cheese,
    shaved in curls

If using dried mushrooms, soak in cold water for
1–2 hours, then drain and check that no sand or dirt
remains. Place in a saucepan with as little water as
possible, acidulated with a small squeeze of lemon
juice. Bring to the boil, then simmer until tender.
Drain, reserving the cooking liquid. Return the liquid
to the pan and boil to reduce to a couple of teaspoons.
Add the truffle oil.

If using fresh mushrooms, trim the stalks and clean
with a brush. Rinse them only if they are dirty, then
cut into pieces if they are large. Sauté in a little grapeseed oil, adding salt and pepper. When cooked, add the
truffle oil.

Cook the pasta in plenty of boiling salted water until
just tender but still firm to the bite (al dente). Drain,
coat with a little grapeseed oil, then leave to cool but
do not chill.

Mix the mushrooms with the pasta, season well and
garnish with curls of Parmesan.

*Serve as a first course, followed by breadcrumbed escalopes
of veal with asparagus.*

Flower power

SERVES 4–6

a selection of edible flowers
  (chive, lavender, thyme,
  borage, strawberry, viola,
  nasturtium, fennel, marigold)
a selection of leaves (fennel,
  tarragon, chervil, nasturtium,
  flat-leaf parsley)
200 g/7 oz mixed baby salad
  leaves

Dressing

2 tablespoons clear honey
4 tablespoons grapeseed oil
2 tablespoons white wine vinegar
chopped fresh tarragon or chervil
salt and pepper

Mix together all the ingredients for the mustard-free vinaigrette and season to taste. Alternatively, make an orange vinaigrette (page 35).

Divide up the flower heads of chive, lavender and thyme into individual florets. Borage, strawberry and viola can be left whole, the others torn into petals.

Arrange the leaves and flowers in a bowl and serve the dressing separately.

Serve as an accompaniment to any light summer meal such as poached salmon with sorrel sauce.

RED BEET CHARD SALAD

SERVES 4

500 g/1 lb 2 oz red beet chard*
    leaves and stalks
freshly grated nutmeg
225 g/8 oz canned water
    chestnuts, rinsed and drained
toasted sesame seeds

Dressing

½ tablespoon Dijon mustard
1 tablespoon red wine vinegar
3 tablespoons vegetable oil
3 tablespoons sesame seed oil
salt and pepper

*This also works very well with
green chard, but Swiss chard,
with its huge white stalks, is
not suitable for this salad.*

Mix the ingredients for the dressing together and season to taste.

Cook the chard in plenty of salted boiling water until cooked but still firm.

Drain well, squeezing out the excess liquid with a clean tea towel if necessary: it must not ooze water. Chop roughly and season with plenty of nutmeg, salt and pepper.

Cut the chestnuts into quarters and mix with the chard. Toss in the dressing, ensuring the chard is well coated, taste and adjust the seasoning and leave to cool.

Serve sprinkled with sesame seeds.

Serve as a salad accompaniment to a variety of cold meats and salami with a sweet red onion confit.

MIXED GRILLED VEGETABLE SALAD

SERVES 6–8

½ each of red, green and yellow
    pepper, seeds removed, cut
    into six
1 courgette, cut into thick rounds
½ aubergine, sliced into rounds
4 tablespoons olive oil
¼ small celeriac, cut into batons
10 button mushrooms, quartered
salt and pepper
2 tablespoons balsamic vinegar

Marinade
150 ml/5 fl oz olive oil
1 sprig of rosemary
1 sprig of thyme
1 garlic clove, chopped
1 shallot, chopped
2 tablespoons sherry vinegar

Place all the marinade ingredients in a saucepan and heat through.

Heat a chargrilling pan, add the peppers, allow to blacken a little, then remove and set aside. Brown the courgette and aubergine rounds in the same way. Add to the peppers.

Heat the olive oil in a large frying pan, add the celeriac and mushrooms and cook briefly to soften a little. Add the peppers, courgette and aubergine, stir in the marinade and season to taste. Pour into a bowl, add the balsamic vinegar and leave to marinate overnight in the refrigerator.

To serve, remove the rosemary and thyme sprigs and drain off excess oil.

Serve as an accompaniment to grilled lamb cutlets.

The Basics

VINEGARS AND OILS

A simple vinaigrette has two main ingredients, oil and vinegar, with an emulsifier – usually a mustard, but it can be sugar or honey – to hold them together. Since these ingredients come in many flavours, the combinations are endless.

VINEGARS

These can be made from wines, cider, malts, rice – in fact almost anything that can or has produced an alcohol by fermentation.

Vinegars are sometimes flavoured by infusing or macerating herbs, such as tarragon, or fruit, such as raspberry or lemon. The result is a powerful source of flavouring and should be used with discretion.

Balsamic vinegar is made from Trebbiano grape juice matured in wooden barrels. These give it its dark colour and distinctive, slightly sweet flavour. It is much less pungent than other vinegars.

Oils

Culinary oils are pressed from nuts, vegetables and fruits. They have a wide range of viscosities, and this is an important consideration when they are to be served cold. For example, olive oil becomes thick and heavy, while grapeseed oil remains liquid and light.

Mixing a delicate or neutral flavoured oil, such as groundnut (peanut), with a strong one like hazelnut can vary the strength of a dressing. The better quality and fresher the oil, the better the flavour.

When making dressings, a proportion of 4:1 oil to vinegar is the norm. However, when using a Dijon mustard, which has wine vinegar among its ingredients, the quantity of oil should be increased.

Orange vinaigrette

150 g/5 oz sugar
150 ml/5 fl oz vinegar
grated zest of 1 orange
1 teaspoon Dijon mustard
150 ml/5 fl oz groundnut oil

Put the sugar in a saucepan with 4 tablespoons water. Heat gently until dissolved, then bring to the boil and allow to caramelize. Add the vinegar and the orange zest and boil to reduce to about 150 ml/5 fl oz.

Put the mustard in a bowl, blend in the orange vinegar mixture and whisk in the oil. Leave to cool.

Use this sweet-and-sour dressing with a mixed leaf and flower salad (page 28). It is also delicious with a hot goats' cheese salad.

TO SKIN AND SEED
TOMATOES

Using a small sharp knife, cut a cross in the stem scar of each tomato. Drop them into a saucepan of fast-boiling water. Count to 13, then drain the tomatoes and refresh in cold water. Peel off the skins. Cut the tomatoes in half and scoop out the seeds with a teaspoon.

TO SEGMENT CITRUS
FRUIT

Using a sharp knife, cut a slice from the top and bottom of the fruit, right through to the flesh. Cut away the skin and pith, working from top to bottom, following the curve of the fruit.

Holding the fruit in the palm of one hand over a bowl to catch the juice, cut down between the membrane and the orange segment. As you reach the centre of the fruit, twist the knife and cut up the other side of the segment, letting the piece fall into the bowl. Repeat with the remaining segments, turning back the flaps of membrane like the pages of a book.

TO KEEP HERBS FRESH

There is a wide selection of fresh herbs available in most supermarkets these days. However, unless used quickly they soon lose their freshness and wilt. To extend their life, rinse in cold water and cut off the bottom of the stems. Stand the stems in a small jar of cold water and tie a polythene bag loosely over the top. Keep in a cool place, changing the water every couple of days. This method is especially effective with coriander.

Classic Cooking

STARTERS
Jean Christophe Novelli Chef/patron of Maison Novelli, which opened in London to great acclaim in 1996. He previously worked at the Four Seasons restaurant, London.

VEGETABLE SOUPS
Elisabeth Luard Cookery writer for the *Sunday Telegraph Magazine* and author of *European Peasant Food* and *European Festival Food*, which won a Glenfiddich Award.

GOURMET SALADS
Sonia Stevenson The first woman chef in the UK to be awarded a Michelin star, at the Horn of Plenty in Devon. Author of *The Magic of Saucery* and *Fresh Ways with Fish*.

FISH AND SHELLFISH
Gordon Ramsay Chef/proprietor of one of London's most popular restaurants, Aubergine, recently awarded its second Michelin star. He is the author of *A Passion for Flavour*.

CHICKEN, DUCK AND GAME
Nick Nairn Chef/patron of Braeval restaurant near Aberfoyle in Scotland, whose BBC-TV series *Wild Harvest* was last summer's most successful cookery series, accompanied by a book.

LIVERS, SWEETBREADS AND KIDNEYS
Simon Hopkinson Former chef/patron at London's Bibendum restaurant, columnist and author of *Roast Chicken and Other Stories* and the forthcoming *The Prawn Cocktail Years*.

VEGETARIAN
Rosamond Richardson Author of several vegetarian titles, including *The Great Green Gourmet* and *Food from Green Places*. She has also appeared on television.

PASTA
Joy Davies One of the creators of *BBC Good Food Magazine*, she has been food editor of *She, Woman* and *Options* and written for the *Guardian, Daily Telegraph* and *Harpers & Queen*.

CHEESE DISHES
Rose Elliot The UK's most successful vegetarian cookery writer and author of many books, including *Not Just a Load of Old Lentils* and *The Classic Vegetarian Cookbook*.

POTATO DISHES
Patrick McDonald Author of the forthcoming *Simply Good Food* and Harvey Nichols' food consultant.

BISTRO COOKING
Anne Willan Founder and director of La Varenne Cookery School in Burgundy and West Virginia. Author of many books and a specialist in French cuisine.

ITALIAN COOKING
Anna Del Conte is the author of *The Classic Food of Northern Italy* (chosen as the 1996 Guild of Food Writers Book of the Year) and *The Gastronomy of Italy*. She has appeared on BBC-TV's *Masterchef*.

VIETNAMESE COOKING
Nicole Routhier One of the United States' most popular cookery writers, her books include *Cooking Under Wraps*, *Nicole Routhier's Fruit Cookbook* and the award-winning *The Foods of Vietnam*.

MALAYSIAN COOKING
Jill Dupleix One of Australia's best known cookery writers, with columns in the *Sydney Morning Herald* and *Elle*. Author of *New Food*, *Allegro al dente* and the Master Chefs *Pacific*.

PEKING CUISINE
Helen Chen Learned to cook traditional Peking dishes from her mother, Joyce Chen, the grande dame of Chinese cooking in the United States. The author of *Chinese Home Cooking*.

STIR FRIES
Kay Fairfax Author of several books, including *100 Great Stir-fries*, *Homemade* and *The Australian Christmas Book*.

NOODLES
Terry Durack Australia's most widely read restaurant critic and co-editor of the *Sydney Morning Herald Good Food Guide*. He is the author of *YUM!*, a book of stories and recipes.

NORTH INDIAN CURRIES
Pat Chapman Started the Curry Club in 1982. Appears regularly on television and radio and is the author of eighteen books, the latest being *The Thai Restaurant Cookbook*.

BARBECUES AND GRILLS
Brian Turner Chef/patron of Turner's in Knightsbridge and one of Britain's most popular food broadcasters; he appears frequently on *Ready Steady Cook*, *Food and Drink* and many other television programmes.

SUMMER AND WINTER CASSEROLES
Anton Edelmann Maître Chef des Cuisines at the Savoy Hotel, London, and author of six books. He appears regularly on BBC-TV's *Masterchef*.

TRADITIONAL PUDDINGS
Tessa Bramley Chef/patron of the acclaimed Old Vicarage restaurant in Ridgeway, Derbyshire. Author of *The Instinctive Cook*, and a regular presenter on a new Channel 4 daytime series *Here's One I Made Earlier*.

DECORATED CAKES
Jane Asher Author of several cookery books and a novel. She has also appeared in her own television series, *Jane Asher's Christmas* (1995).

FAVOURITE CAKES
Mary Berry One of Britain's leading cookery writers, her numerous books include *Mary Berry's Ultimate Cake Book*. She has made many television and radio appearances and is a regular contributor to cookery magazines.

First published in 1997 by
George Weidenfeld & Nicolson
The Orion Publishing Group
Orion House
5 Upper St Martin's Lane
London WC2H 9EA

British Library Cataloguing-in-Publication data
A catalogue record for this book is available from
the British Library

ISBN 0 297 82283 7

Designed by Lucy Holmes
Edited by Maggie Ramsay
Food styling by Joy Davies
Typeset by Tiger Typeset